THE EPIC OF GILGAMESH

Translation by A. Snow

D1713297

ISBN 9798773322528

Contents

Introduction

The Epic of Gilgamesh is an epic poem of Sumerian origin, written in cuneiform characters on clay tablets, which dates back to about 4,500 years ago between 2,600 BC and 2,500 BC. There are six known versions of poems that narrate the exploits of Gilgamesh, Sumerian king of Uruk, grandson of Enmerkar and son of Lugalbanda. The best known version, the so-called *Epic of Gilgamesh* is Babylonian. It is one of the oldest known poems and tells the deeds of an ancient and legendary Sumerian king, Gilgamesh, grappling with the problem that has always plagued humanity: death and its impossible overcoming. The epic (or more simply "the Gilgamesh") predates the Homeric poems (VIII century BC) and the Indian Vedas (1,500 BC). The earliest Sumerian drafting of the poem can be traced back to over 2,000 BC. Documents on Gilgamesh have been found more or less everywhere in Mesopotamia, but also outside, as in Anatolia (Hattusa, capital of the Hittite empire) or in Palestine (Megiddo).

The Epic of Gilgamesh collects all those writings that discuss the exploits of the mythical king of Uruk and has to be considered as the most important of the Babylonian and Assyrian mythological texts that have been handed down to us. In addition to the main edition, set up for the library of King Ashurbanipal and now kept in the British Museum in London, there are other older and fragmentary versions of this work. All peoples who have come into contact with the Sumerian world have felt the greatness of inspiration, so much so that cuneiform tablets with the text of Gilgameš have been found in Anatolia, written in the Hittite and Hurrian languages, and in Syria-Israel. The oldest texts dealing with the hero's adventures belong to Sumerian literature and scenes from the epic are found, as well as on various bas-reliefs, on cylindrical seals from the third millennium BC.

The Epic of Gilgamesh was discovered in 1853 by the Assyrian archaeologist Hormuzd Rassam. In 1870, an English translation was published by the Assyrologist George Smith, which was followed by other translations into various modern languages. The most recent and complete critical version in English is a two-volume book published in 2004 by Andrew George and which includes the exegesis of each individual tablet with the original text and facing translation. The first version in Arabic directly from the original tablets dates back to 1960 by the Iraqi archaeologist Taha Baqir.

The discovery of some artifacts dated to 2600 BC which refer to Enmebaragesi king of Kish, mentioned in the epic as the father of one of Gilgamesh's opponents, has strengthened the credibility of Gilgamesh's actual historical existence.

HISTORICAL SOURCES

The sources of the epic are various and cover a period of about two thousand years. The original Sumerian poems and the subsequent Akkadian language version are the main sources of modern translations; the older Sumerian version is mainly used to fill in the gaps in the Akkadian version. Despite recent additions, the epic still remains incomplete.

The earliest core of Sumerian poems is modernly regarded as a collection of separate stories, rather than a single unitary epic. The origin dates back to the third dynasty of Ur (2,150-2,000 BC), while the oldest Akkadian versions are dated to the beginning of the second millennium BC, probably between the eighteenth and seventeenth centuries BC. when some authors used existing literary material to shape a unified epic. The Akkadian standard version, which consists of twelve clay tablets, was written by Sin-liqe-unninni, between 1,300 and 1,000 BC. and was found in Ashurbanipal's library in Nineveh.

It corresponds to the so-called Classical epic or Nineveh epic. The name originates from the place where it was found: Nineveh, capital of the Assyrian Empire, where one of the major libraries of antiquity was located: the library of Ashurbanipal. This editing is the longest, the most complex and the best preserved to date. In fact, the Gilgamesh is not a complete work. The documents at our disposal are often fragmentary, written in different languages, belonging to different epochs, and with a content that is not always homogeneous. The texts were written in cuneiform, writing more suited to the type of final support, clay modeled in the form of a tablet. Despite the shortcomings, the overall picture of the work has now been clarified and constant archaeological discoveries allow us to add new pieces to both the Nineveh epic and the older versions, including those from the Sumerian era. The classic epic dates back to around 1,200 BC. but it has reached us in the later Neo-Assyrian redaction (ca. 700 BC). It is composed of twelve chapters written in Akkadian (not Sumerian, although places and characters are distinctly Sumerian) on as many tablets. The classic epic is the result of a literary elaboration dating back to the dawn of writing, divided into 4 parts:

Part 1: the Sumerian poems. These poems written in Sumerian date back to the third millennium BC and present, independently of one another, various themes that will converge in the classical epic. They did not constitute a unitary epic corpus. In fact, Gilgamesh, if he appears, impersonates various roles (adventurer, ruler of Uruk, judge of the afterlife, brother of Ishtar goddess of love, etc.).

Part 2: the Old-Babylonian poem. The first real attempt at a unitary epic composition on the deeds of the king of Uruk took place around 1,800-1,600 BC, or at the time of the first dynasty of Babylon with his prestigious king. Hammurabi known for the "first" code of laws (the first codes are actually from the Sumerian era). This saga is called the Old-Babylonian poem of Gilgamesh. From the poem of Gilgamesh these splendid verses are taken that admonish the protagonist obsessed with the search for immortality: "Gilgamesh, where are you going? The life you seek, you will not find it. When the gods created humanity, they assigned death to it, and they kept life for themselves! Fill your stomach, Gilgamesh. Party day and night, your clothes are clean! Wash your garment, wash yourself with water! Rejoice in the child who holds your hand, may your wife enjoy you. This is the destiny of men! ". These are practically the last lines of what is left of the Gilgamesh poem. The protagonist, wandering in search of the secret to escape death, is admonished by Siduri, the tavern-keeper of Shamash (god of justice) for neglecting the exercise of power looking for a chimera. We do not know if the poem contained the narrative of the flood but it is certain that it at least contained Gilgamesh's encounter with the distant ancestor who survived the Flood.

Part 3: the Middle Babylonian sagas and the myth of Atra-Hasis. The later sagas written in extra-Babylonian languages (Hittite, Elamic,

Khurrian) and found in Anatolia, Syria, Israel will be inspired by the poem of Gilgamesh as evidence of the enormous fortune of the poem in antiquity. These date back to the Babylonian period (14th-12th century BC) and contain one more "detail" than the poem: the entire narrative of the universal flood. This version is incredibly similar to the one we find in Genesis. The Mid-Babylonian sagas are more or less equivalent in content but are very different in form. We have, for example, sagas in different languages, sagas in prose, others in verse, or with a variable extension from one to another.

Part 4: the Classical Babylonian The title commonly assigned to this work, The Epic of Gilgamesh, is modern and in no way attributable to its authors. This version, indicated by moderns as "classical", is attributed to the scribe and exorcist Cassite Sîn-lēqi-unninni and was found in clay fragments among the ruins of the royal library in the palace of King Ashurbanipal in Nineveh, capital of Assyrian empire. This work was certainly collected and canonized before the 8th century BC, perhaps around the 12th century BC, and subsequently faithfully reproduced as was the custom of the scribes.

In summary, the literary phases that will lead to the epic of Gilgamesh are the following:
Sumerian poems (2,500 BC) Old-Babylonian poem of Gilgamesh (1,700 BC) Mid-Babylonian sagas of Gilgamesh and the Great Sage's poem (1,200 BC.) Around the 12th century BC the literary material (epic and mythological) is ready for a new rearrangement. Perhaps precisely in this period, at the latest a century later, the verse compilation of the adventures of Gilgamesh took place according to a unitary structure, which has come down to us in the late Assyrian version (8th century BC).

PLOT

The title assigned by modern scholars to the narrative derives from the name of the protagonist, Gilgamesh, the Sumerian king of Uruk (Erech in the Bible, currently Tell-al-Warka in Iraq), a hero who faces adventures of all kinds and, after the death of the Comrade Enkidu, set out in search of the secret of immortality.

Gilgamesh is the Sumerian king of the city of Uruk. A cruel warrior, he is two thirds divine and one third mortal and he holds under his dominion a people increasingly tired of his bullying and injustices. The gods, therefore, to punish him, decide to create a man capable of opposing him, Enkidu. He is primitive and rough, molded from clay and described in the epic as wild both in physique and behavior.

The two clash, as expected, but the clash ends evenly. Struck by the strength of Enkidu, Gilgamesh makes a pact of friendship with him. They decide to go together to the Cedar Forest to collect the precious wood of these trees. However, guarding the forest there is a monster, Humbaba, which the two manage to defeat without major problems.

Increased further his fame and friendship with Enkidu, Gilgamesh is courted by Ishtar (the goddess of beauty and fertility, but also of war and destruction), who would like him as a husband, delighted by his skills as a warrior and fame. of him. Gilgamesh, however, rejects it, given the sad fate of the goddess's past lovers, such as Dumuzi, Isullanu, etc. Ishtar fell prey to bitter anger and asked his father Anu (the god of Heaven and father of Ishtar herself) to give him the bull of the sky and her father granted it to him.+Ishtar led the bull to Uruk and the animal caused the death of hordes of young people, so Enkidu grabbed the bull by the horns and Gilgamesh slipped his sword between the horns, killing him. Ishtar climbed the great wall of Uruk and cursed Gilgamesh, who exposed the bull's horns in the palace and with Enkidu walked through the streets of the city, who celebrated and celebrated the event. The next day Enkidu, after waking up, told Gilgamesh the dream he had had in which the gods had decreed his death. In fact, soon Enkidu was seized by a serious illness which led to his death after ten days. Gilgamesh made a speech to the advisers of Uruk that reminded them of his friendship with Enkidu and made them share in his pain, finally arranged for a statue to be made in memory of his unforgettable friend.

Gilgamesh wept and wandered desperately through the moors and plains, finally decided to go in search of Utnapistim, the one they call the Far, the one the gods had taken with them after the Great Flood and had placed him to live in the land of Dilmun, and, to him alone, they had given immortality. Gilgamesh, in order to bring his friend Enkidu back to life, would like to obtain from Utnapistim the secret of his life. Gilgamesh then reaches the great Mashu mountains, whose peaks are as high as the wall of heaven and his knolls descend down to the underworld, at his gates the scorpion men guard. The scorpion man allowed him to cross the mountain gate, something that had never been granted to any mortal. After traveling twelve leagues completely in the dark, Gilgmesh arrives at the garden of the gods. While he was walking in the garden he was seen by Šamaš who said to him: You will never find the life you are looking for. Gilgmesh continues his journey and meets Siduri who at first tries to avoid him, but Gilgamesh, revealing her identity to him, asks him to open the door of his house, and confides that he is trying to overcome the fear of death. But Siduri confirms what Šamaš said and advises him to enjoy the pleasures of life. But Gilgmesh wants to continue the search for her and asks the girl to show him the way to reach the place where Utnapistim (Paradise) lives. Siduri advises him not to continue as no man has ever managed to cross the ocean, however he directs him to Urshanabi, the boatman of Utnapistim, telling him that perhaps there is the possibility that he will accompany him, otherwise he will have to give up on the undertaking. In anger, Gilgmesh and destroys the rigging of Urshanabi's boat who, after seeing him in action, approached him and made his name known, as did Gilgames. Gilgamesh's disappointment is, however, great: the sage replies that death is inevitable for the man who, sooner or later, will have to leave this world. Gilgamesh, now hopeless, is about to leave when Utanapishtim, pitying, reveals to him that there is only one possibility for eternal youth: it is a plant found at the bottom of the sea. Gilgamesh immediately sets out in search of the precious vegetable and, after having found it, decides to rest on the banks of a stream. Upon awakening, he discovers that the precious plant has been eaten by a snake, which after eating it has shed its skin. Defeated, he returns to Uruk, his city. Gilgamesh begs the god of the underworld to make him see Enkidu one last time. The wish is granted and the soul of the latter is presented to Gilgamesh. Enkidu reveals to his great friend that life in the afterlife is sad and gloomy, full of regrets for all that has not been done in earthly life and for the opportunities that have been missed. He therefore advises him to leave the dead alone and to enjoy life as long as possible, given that in the afterlife, existence will be flat and without happiness. The only people who will be able to enjoy a dignified existence in the afterlife are those who have generated numerous children, mirroring the concept that the only way to live forever is to leave offspring.

PROLOGUE: GILGAMESH KING IN URUK

I will proclaim the deeds of Gilgamesh to the world. This was the man to whom all things were known; this was the king who knew the countries of the world. He was wise, he saw mysteries and knew secret things, he brought us a tale of the days before the flood. He went a long way, he was tired, exhausted from work, returning he rested, engraved the whole story on a stone.

When the gods created Gilgamesh they gave him a perfect body. Shamash the glorious sun endowed him with beauty, Adad the storm god endowed him with courage, the great gods made his beauty perfect, surpassing all others, terrifying as a great wild bull. For two thirds they made him god and for a third man.

In Uruk he built walls, a great bastion and the temple of blessed Eanna for the god of the firmament Anu, and for Ishtar the goddess of love. Look at it still today: the outer wall where the cornice runs, shines with the brilliance of copper; and the inner wall has no equal. Touch the threshold, it is ancient. Approach Eanna the abode of Ishtar, our lady of love and war, as no king of the last days, no living man can match. Climb the wall of Uruk; walk along it, I say; consider the foundation terrace and examine the masonry: isn't it burned brick and good? The seven wise men laid the foundation.

THE COMING OF ENKIDU

Gilgamesh went abroad to the world, but met no one who could resist his arms until he came to Uruk. But the men of Uruk murmured in their homes, "Gilgamesh plays the tocsin for his amusement, his arrogance has no limits by day or night. No son is left with his father, as Gilgamesh takes them all, even the children; yet the king should be a shepherd to his people. His lust leaves no virgin to her lover, neither the warrior's daughter nor her wife of the nobleman; yet this is the shepherd of the city, wise, handsome and resolute."

The gods heard their lament, the gods of the sky cried out to the Lord of Uruk, to Anu the god of Uruk: "A goddess made him, strong as a wild bull, no one can resist his arms. No child remained with his father, because Gilgamesh takes them all; and is this the king, the shepherd of his people? His lust for no virgin to her lover, neither the warrior's daughter nor the nobleman's wife." When Anu had heard their lament, the gods shouted to Aruru, the goddess of creation, "You created him, O Aruru; now create his equal; let it be like him as his own reflection, his second self; stormy heart for stormy heart. Let them fight together and leave Uruk in silence."

Thus the goddess conceived an image in her mind, and it was of the stuff of Anuf the firmament. She dipped her hands in the water and removed the clay, dropped it into the wilderness and the noble Enkidu was created. There was in him the virtue of the god of war, of Ninurta himself. His body was rough, his hair was long like a woman's; it waved like the hair of Nisaba, the goddess of wheat. His body was covered with hair clipped like that of Samugan, the god of cattle. He was innocent of humanity; he knew nothing of the cultivated land.

Enkidu ate the grass on the hills with the gazelle and lurked with the wild beasts at the pools of water; he enjoyed the water with the herds of game.

But there was a trapper who one day met him face to face at the water-trough, because the game had entered his territory. For three days he met him face to face and the trapper was frozen with fear. He returned to his house with the game he had caught, and was speechless, numb with terror.

His face was as altered as that of someone who has traveled a long way. With awe in his heart he spoke to his father: "Father, there is a man, different from all others, coming down from the hills. He is the strongest in the world, he is like an immortal from heaven. He sweeps the hills with wild beasts and eats grass; he walks your land and goes down to the wells. I am afraid and I do not dare to go near him. He fills the pits that I dig and tears apart my game traps; he helps the beasts escape and now they slip through my fingers."

His father opened his mouth and said to the trapper: "My son, Gilgamesh lives in Uruk; no one has ever prevailed against him, he is as strong as a star in the sky. Go to Uruk, find Gilgamesh, exalt the strength of this savage man. Ask him to give you a harlot, a lascivious one from the temple of love; return with her, and let her woman's power override this man. When next he comes down to drink at the wells she will be there, naked; and when he sees her, she beckons for him, he will embrace her, and then the beasts will reject him."

So the hunter set out for Uruk and turned to Gilgamesh saying: "A man different from the rest is now wandering in the pastures; he is strong as a star in the sky and I am afraid to get close to him. He helps the game escape; he fills my pits and pulls up my traps." Gilgamesh said, "Trapper, go back, take a prostitute with you, a child of pleasure. At the drinking hole she will strip, and when he sees her beckoning, he will hug her and the game of the wilderness will surely reject him."

Now the trapper returned, taking the prostitute with him. After three days of traveling they came to the drinking hole, and there they sat down; the harlot and the trapper sat facing each other and waiting for the game to arrive. For the first day and for the second day the two sat and waited, but on the third day the herds came; they went down to drink and Enkidu was with them. The little wild creatures of the plains were content with the water, and Enkidu with them, who ate the grass with the gazelle and was born in the hills; and she saw him, the savage, coming from afar to the hills. The trapper spoke to her: "Here he is. Now, woman, bare your breasts, do not be ashamed, do not delay but welcome his love. Show him yourself naked, let him possess your body. When he gets close, uncover yourself and lie down with him; teach him, the savage, the art of a woman, because when he murmurs love to you, the "wild beasts that have shared his life with him in the hills will reject him."

She was not ashamed to take him, she undressed and accepted his eagerness; as he lay upon her murmuring love, she taught him the art of woman. For six days and seven nights they were together, for Enkidu had forgotten his home in the hills; but when he was satisfied he returned to the wild beasts. Then, when the gazelle saw him, they ran away; when the wild creatures saw him they fled. Enkidu would follow him, but his body was as if tied with a rope, his knees gave way as he started to run, his speed was gone. And now the wild creatures had all fled; Enkidu had become weak, because wisdom was in him, and a man's thoughts were in his heart. So he came back and sat down at the woman's feet, and listened carefully to what she said. "You are wise, Enkidu, and now you have become like a god. Why do you want to run wild with the beasts in the hills? Come with me. I will take you to the sturdy walled Uruk, to the blessed temple of Ishtar and Anu, of love and heaven, there lives Gilgamesh, who is very strong and like a wild bull he rules over men."

When she spoke, Enkidu was pleased; he wanted a companion, one who would understand his heart. "Come, woman, and take me to that sacred temple, to the house of Anu and Ishtar, and to the place where Gilgamesh is the lord of people. I will challenge him boldly, I will shout loudly in Uruk: 'I am the strongest here, I have come to change the old order, I am the one who was born in the hills, I am the strongest of all.' "

She said, "Let's go, and show him your face. I know very well where Gilgamesh is in great Uruk. O Enkidu, there all the people are dressed in their beautiful clothes, every day is a holiday, the young men and girls are wonderful to see. What a scent they have! All the great ones are awakened from their beds. O Enkidu, you who love life, I will show you Gilgamesh, a man of many humors; you will look at him well in his radiant manhood. His body is perfect in strength and maturity; he never rests at night or during the day. He is stronger than you, so leave your boasting. Shamash the glorious sun gave favors to Gilgamesh, and Anu of the heavens, and Enlil, and Ea the wise gave him deep understanding, I tell you, even before you have left the wilderness, Gilgamesh will know in his dreams that you are arriving."

Now Gilgamesh rose to tell his dream to his mother; Ninsun, one of the wise gods. "Mom, last night I had a dream. I was filled with joy, the young heroes were around me and I walked into the night under the stars of firmament, and one, a meteor of the matter of Anu, fell from the sky. I tried to lift it but it turned out to be too heavy. All the people of Uruk came to see it, the common people flocked and the nobles flocked to kiss its feet; and its attraction to me was like a woman's love. They helped me, I braced my forehead and lifted it with thongs and I brought it to you and you yourself pronounced it my brother".

Then Ninsun, who is beloved and wise, said to Gilgamesh: "This star of heaven has come down from heaven like a meteor; that you tried to lift, but you found it too heavy, when you tried to move it did not move, and so you brought it to my feet; I did it for you, a goad and a spur, and you were drawn as for a woman. This is the strong companion, the one who brings help to his friend in his need. He is the strongest of wild creatures, the stuff of Anu; born in the wild grasslands and hills raised him; when you see him you will rejoice; you will love him as a woman and he will never abandon you. This is the meaning of the dream."

Gilgamesh said, "Mom, I had a second dream. There was an ax in the sturdy-walled streets of Uruk; the shape was strange and people crowded around. I saw it and I was happy with it. I bent down, deeply attracted to it; I loved it like a woman and carried it by my side." Ninsun replied: "That ax, which you saw, which drew you as powerfully as a woman's love, this is the companion I give you, and he will come in his strength as one of the army of heaven. He is the brave companion who saves his friend in need." Gilgamesh said to his mother about him: "A friend, a counselor has come to me from Enlil, and now I will befriend and advise him." So Gilgamesh told his dreams; and the harlot retold them to Enkidu.

And now he said to Enkidu: "When I look at you you have become like a god. Why do you long to run wild again with the beasts in the hills? Get up off the ground, shepherd's bed." He listened carefully to her words. What she gave was good advice. She divided her robes in two and with her half dressed him and with the the other herself, and holding him by her hand she led him like a child to the folds, in the shepherds' tents. There all the shepherds flocked to see him, they placed bread in front of him, but Enkidu could only suck the milk of wild beasts. He fumbled and gasped, not knowing what to do or how he should eat the bread and drink the strong wine. Then the woman said, "Enkidu, eat the bread, it is the staff of life; drinking wine is the custom of the earth." So he ate until he was satisfied and drank strong wine, seven cups. He became cheerful, his heart rejoiced and his face shone. He rubbed the tousled hair of his body and anointed himself with oil. Enkidu had become a man; but when he was dressed as a man, he appeared as a bridegroom. He took up arms to hunt the lion so that the shepherds could rest at night. He captured wolves and lions and the shepherds lay down in peace; because Enkidu was their guardian, that strong man that was unrivaled.

He was happily living with the shepherds, until one day looking up he saw a man approaching. He said to the prostitute: "Woman, bring that man here. Why did he come? I would like to know his name." She went and called the man saying, "Lord, where are you going on this grueling journey?" The man replied, saying to Enkidu, "Gilgamesh has entered the wedding house and has shut the people out. He does strange things in Umk, the city of great streets. At the roll of the drum begins the work for the men, and the work for the women. King Gilgamesh is about to celebrate marriage to the Queen of Love, and he still claims to be first with the bride, the king to be first and husband to follow, because this has been ordained by the gods since his birth, by the time the umbilical cord was cut. But now the drums roll for the choice of the bride and the city groans." At these words Enkidu turned pale. "I will go to the place where Gilgamesh dominates the people, bravely challenge him and shout loudly in Uruk: 'I have come to change the old order, because here I am the strongest.'"

Now Enkidu walked ahead and the woman followed him. He went into Umk, that big market, and all the people crowded around him where he stood on the street in sturdy walled Umk. People bumped; speaking of him they said: "He is the spit of Gilgamesh". "He is shorter." "He is bigger of bone." "This is the one that was raised with the milk of wild beasts. His is the greatest strength." The men rejoiced: "Now Gilgamesh has met his match. This great one, this hero whose beauty is like a god, he is a match even for Gilgamesh."

In Umk the wedding bed was made, suitable for the goddess of love. The bride was waiting for the bridegroom, but in the night Gilgamesh got up and came to the house. Then Enkidu went out, stopped in the street and blocked the way. The mighty Gilgamesh arrived and Enkidu met him at the door. He stretched out his foot and prevented Gilgamesh from entering the house, so they clung, holding each other like bulls. They broke the doorposts and the walls shook, snorted like bulls locked together. They shattered the doorposts and the walls shook. Gilgamesh bent his knee with his foot planted on the ground and with a twist Enkidu was thrown. Then immediately his fury towards him died. When Enkidu was thrown, he said to Gilgamesh: "There is no other like you in the world. Ninsun, who is strong as a wild ox in the stable, was the mother who gave birth to you, and now you are exalted above all men, and Enlil has given you the kingdom, because your strength surpasses the strength of men." So Enkidu and Gilgamesh embraced and their friendship was sealed.

THE FOREST JOURNEY

Enlil of the mountain, the father of the gods, had decreed the fate of Gilgamesh. So Gilgamesh dreamed and Enkidu said: "The meaning of the dream is this. The father of the gods gave you the kingdom, this is your destiny, eternal life is not your destiny. Therefore do not be sad at heart, do not be grieved or burdened. He has given you the power to bind and untie, to be the darkness and light of humanity. He has given you unrivaled supremacy over the people, a victory in battle from which no fugitive returns, in raids and assaults from which he does not flinch. But do not abuse this power, deal with justice with your servants in the palace, deal with justice before Shamash."

The eyes of Enkidu were filled with tears and his heart was sick. He sighed bitterly and Gilgamesh met his gaze and said, "My friend, why are you sighing so bitterly?" But Enkidu opened his mouth and said: "I am weak, my arms have lost their strength, the cry of pain sticks in my throat, I am oppressed by idleness."

It was then that Lord Gilgamesh turned his thoughts to the Land of the Living; on the Land of Cedars, Lord Gilgamesh reflected. He said to his servant Enkidu: "I have not established my name printed on bricks as my destiny has decreed; therefore I will go to the country where the cedar is cut. I will put my name in the place where the names of famous men are written, and where no man's name is written yet, I will erect a monument to the gods. Because of the evil that is in the earth, we will go to the forest and destroy the evil; because in the forest lives Humbaba whose name is "Hugeness", a ferocious giant." But Enkidu sighed bitterly and said, "When I went with the wild beasts that roamed the wilderness, I discovered the forest; its length is ten thousand leagues in each direction.

Enlil appointed Humbaba to guard it and armed him with three seven-fold terrors, terrible for all flesh is Humbaba. When he roars he is like the torrent of the storm, his breath is like fire and his jaws are death. He guards the cedars so well that when the wild heifer moves through the forest, even though it is sixty leagues away, he hears it.

Which man would gladly enter that country and explore its depths? I tell you, weakness overwhelms those who approach it; it is not an equal fight when fighting with Humbaba; he is a great warrior, a ram. Gilgamesh, the guardian of the forest never sleeps."

Gilgamesh replied: "Where is the man who can climb into heaven? Only the gods live forever with the glorious Shamash, but as for us humans, our days are numbered, our occupations are a breath of wind. How is this, you are already afraid! I will go first although I am your lord, and you can safely say, 'Come on, there is nothing to fear!' Then if I fall I leave behind me a name that lasts; men – they will say about me, 'Gilgamesh fell in battle with the ferocious Humbaba.' Long after the baby is bony in my house, they will say it and remember it." Enkidu spoke again to Gilgamesh, "O my lord, if you enter that country, go to the hero Shamash first, tell the Sun God, because the earth is his. The country where the cedar is cut belongs to Shamash."

Gilgamesh took a kid, white without blemish, and with it a brown one; she held them against his chest, and he carried them into the presence of the sun. He took his silver scepter in his hand and said to the glorious Shamash: 'Iam go to that country, O Shamash, I go; my hands plead, so let it be good for my soul and take me back to Uruk wharf. Grant, I plead, your protection, and may the omen be good. 'The glorious Shamash replied,' Gilgamesh, you are strong, but what is the Land of the Living for you?

Gilgamesh took a kid, white without blemish, and with it a brown one; he held them against his chest of him, and him he brought them into the presence of the sun. He took his silver scepter in his hand and said to the glorious Shamash, "I am going to that country, O Shamash, I am going; my hands supplicate, so let it be well with my soul and bring me back to the quay of Uruk. Grant, I beseech, your protection, and let the omen be good." Glorious Shamash answered, "Gilgamesh, you are strong, but what is the Country of the Living to you?"

"O Shamash, hear me, hear me, Shamash, let my voice be heard. Here in the city man dies oppressed in his heart, man perishes with despair in his heart. I looked over the wall and saw the bodies floating on the river, and this will also be my destiny. Truly I know it is so, because the highest among men cannot reach the heavens, and the greatest cannot embrace the earth. Therefore I would like to enter that country: since I have not established my name imprinted on brick as my destiny has decreed, I will go to the country where the cedar is cut. I will put my name where the names of famous men are written; and where no one's name is written I will raise a monument to the gods." Tears flowed down his face at him and he said, "Alas, it's a long journey I have to make to the Land of Humbaba. If this feat is not to be accomplished, why have you moved me, Shamash, with a restless desire to accomplish it? How can I be successful if you don't help me? If I die in that country I will die without rancor, but if I return I will make a glorious offering of gifts and praise to Shamash."

So Shamash accepted the sacrifice of his tears; as the compassionate man he showed him mercy. He appointed strong allies for Gilgamesh, sons of one mother, and stationed them in the caves of the mountain. The great winds he named: the north wind, the whirlwind, the stone and the icy wind, the storm and the scorching wind. Like vipers, like dragons, like a burning fire, like a serpent that freezes the heart, a destructive flood and the gallows of lightning, such were they and Gilgamesh rejoiced.

He went to the forge and said: "I will give orders to the armorers; they will throw their weapons at us as we watch them." So they gave orders to the armorers and the craftsmen sat down in conference. They went into the woods of the plain and cut willows and box trees; they cast for them axes of nine pounds, and great swords they cast with blades of six pounds each one, with pommels and hilts of thirty pounds. They cast for Gilgamesh the axe 'Power of Heroes' and the bow of Anshan; and Gilgamesh was armed and Enkidu; and the weight of the arms they carried was thirty pounds.

People gathered and councilors in the streets and market square of Uruk; they passed through the door of the seven latches and Gilgamesh spoke to them in the market square: "I, Gilgamesh, am going to see that creature so spoken of, the voice whose name fills the world. I will conquer him in his cedar wood and show the strength of the sons of Uruk, all the world will know. I am committed to this feat: climbing the mountain, cutting down the cedar and leaving a lasting name behind me." The counselors of Uruk in the great market replied: "Gilgamesh, you are young, your courage takes you too far, you cannot know what this enterprise that you plan means. We have heard that Humbaba is not like men who die, his weapons are such that no one can stand against them; the forest extends for ten thousand leagues in every direction; who would gladly go down to explore its depths? As for Humbaba, when he roars he is like the torrent of the storm, his breath is like fire and his jaws are death itself. Why do you long to do this, Gilgamesh? It is not an equal fight when fighting with Humbaba, that ram"

When he heard these words of the counselors Gilgamesh looked at his friend and laughed: "How will I answer them; I must say that I am afraid of Humbaba, I will stay home for the rest of my days?" Then Gilgamesh opened his mouth again and said to Enkidu: "My friend, let's go to the Grand Palace, Egalmah, and stand before Queen Ninsun. Ninsun is wise with a deep knowledge, she will give us advice on the way to go." They took each other by the hand as they went to Egalmah and went to Ninsun, the great queen. Gilgamesh approached, entered the palace and spoke to Ninsun. "Ninsun, you will hear me; I have a long journey to make, in the Land of Humbaba, I must travel an unknown road and fight a strange battle. From the day I go until I return, until I reach the cedar forest and destroy the evil that Shamash abhors, pray for me Shamash."

Ninsun went to her room, put on a dress that suited her body, put on jewels to make her breasts beautiful, put a tiara on her head, and her skirts swept the ground. She then she went up to the altar of the Sun, standing on the roof of the palace; she burned incense and raised her arms to Shamash as the smoke rose: "O Shamash, why did you give this troubled heart to Gilgamesh, my son; why did you give it? You have moved him and now he goes on a long journey to the Land of Humbaba, to travel an unknown road and fight a strange battle. So from the day he leaves until the day he comes back, until he reaches the cedar forest, until he kills Humbaba and he destroys the evil thing that you, Shamash, abhor, don't forget it; but let the dawn, Aya, your dear bride, always remind you, and when the day is over deliver it to the night watchman to protect him from harm." Then Ninsun, the mother of Gilgamesh, extinguished the incense and called Enkidu with this exhortation: "Strong Enkidu, you are not the son of my body, but I will welcome you as my adopted son; you are my other son like the foundlings who take to the temple. Serve Gilgamesh as a foundling serves the temple and the priestess who raised him. In the presence of my women, any devotees and hierophants, I declare it." Then she put-the amulet for a pledge around her neck, and she said to him: "I entrust my son to you; bring him back to me safe and sound."

And now they brought them their weapons, they put into their hands the great swords in their golden scabbards, and the bow and quiver. Gilgamesh took the ax, threw the quiver from his shoulder, and Anshan's bow, and fastened the sword to his belt; and so they were armed and ready for the journey. Now all the people came and pressed on them and said, "When will you return to the city?" The counselors blessed Gilgamesh and warned him: "Don't trust your strength too much, be vigilant, hold back your blows in the beginning. He who goes ahead protects his companion; the good guide who knows the way guards his friend. Let Enkidu lead the way, he knows the way to the forest, he has seen Humbaba and is an expert in battles; let him press first in the passes, let him be watchful and look at himself. Let Enkidu protect his friend, protect his companion, and lead him safely through the pitfalls of the road. O Enkidu, we, the advisers of Uruk, entrust to you our king; bring him back safely to us." Back to Gilgamesh, they said, "May Shamash give you the desire of your heart, may he make you see it with your own eyes the thing accomplished which your lips have spoken; he opens a way for you where it is barred and a way for your feet to travel. May he open the mountains for your crossing, and may the night bring you the blessings of the night, and Lugulbanda, your guardian god, stand by your side for victory. May you have victory in the battle as if you had fought with a child. Wash your feet in the Humbaba River towards which you are going; in the evening dig a well, and let it always be pure water in your water-skin. Offer cold water to Shamash and don't forget Lugulbanda."

Then Enkidu opened his mouth and said, "Come on, there is nothing to fear. Follow me, because I know the place where Humbaba lives and the paths where he walks. Let the advisers come back. There is no reason to fear here." When the counselors heard this, they hastened the hero on his way. "Go, Gilgamesh, may your guardian god protect you along the way and take you safely back to the Uruk wharf."

After twenty leagues they broke their fast; after another thirty leagues they stopped for the night. Fifty leagues covered in one day; in three days they had already traveled as much as in a month and two weeks. They crossed seven mountains before reaching the forest gate. Then Enkidu cried out to Gilgamesh: "Do not go down into the forest; when I opened the gate my hand lost its strength." Gilgamesh replied, "Dear friend, do not speak like a coward. Have we got the better of so many dangers and traveled so far, to finally go back? You, who are tried in wars and battles, hold me tight now and you will not fear the death; hold me by your side and your weakness will pass, the tremor will leave your hand. Would my friend rather stay behind? No, we will descend together into the heart of the forest. Let your courage be awakened by the battle to come; forget death and follow me, a man determined in action, but not reckless. When two go together, each will protect himself and shield his companion, and if they fall they leave a lasting name."

Together they went down into the forest and came to the green mountain. There they remained motionless, they were speechless; they stopped and looked at the forest. They saw the height of the cedar, they saw the road in the forest and the path where Humbaba used to walk. The road was wide and the path was good. They looked at the cedar mountain, the abode of the gods and the throne of Ishtar. The immensity of the cedar stood in front of the mountain, its shadow was beautiful, full of comfort; mountains and glade were green with brushwood:

There Gilgamesh dug a well before sunset. He went up the mountain, poured good food on the ground and said: "O mountain, abode of the gods, give me a propitious dream." Then they took hands and went to sleep; and the sleep that flows from the night lapped them. Gilgamesh dreamed, and at midnight sleep left him, and he related his dream to his friend. "Enkidu, what woke me up if you didn't? My friend, I dreamed a dream. Get up, look at the precipice of the mountain. The sleep that the gods sent me is broken. Ah, my friend, what a dream I had! Terror and confusion; I grabbed a wild bull in the wilderness. He screamed and beat the dust until the whole sky was dark, my arm was grabbed and my tongue bit. I fell to my knees; then someone refreshed me with the water from his water-skin."

Enkidu said, "Dear friend, the god to whom we are traveling is not a wild bull, although his form is mysterious. That wild bull you have seen is Shamash the Protector; in our moment of danger he will take us by the hand. He who gave water from his water-skin, that is your god who takes care of your good name, your Lugulbanda. United with him, together we will accomplish a feat whose fame will never die."

Gilgamesh said, "I have dreamed again. We were in a deep gorge in the mountain, and beside it the two of us were like the smallest marsh flies; and suddenly the mountain fell, hit me and tore my feet from underneath. Then an intolerable light was emitted, and in it was one whose grace and beauty were greater than beauty of this world. He pulled me out from under the mountain, gave me a drink and my heart was consoled, and he put my feet on the ground."

Then Enkidu, the child of the plains, said, "Let's go down the mountain and talk about this together." He said to Gilgamesh the young god: "Your dream is good, your dream is excellent, the mountain you have seen is Humbaba. Now, of course, we will catch him and kill him, and throw his body to the ground as the mountain fell to the plain."

The next day, after twenty leagues, they broke their fast and after another thirty they stopped for the night. They dug a well before the sun set and Gilgamesh went up the mountain. He poured some good food on the ground and said: "O mountain, abode of the gods, send a dream to Enkidu, make him a propitious dream." The mountain had shaped a dream for Enkidu; it came, a disturbing dream; a cold shower swept over him, made him curl up like mountain barley in a rainstorm. But Gilgamesh sat with his chin on his knees until the sleep that flows over all mankind lapped upon him. Then, at midnight, sleep left him; he got up and said to his friend: "Did you call me or why did I wake up? Did you touch me or why am I terrified? Hasn't some god passed by, why are my limbs numb with fear? My friend, I saw a third dream and this dream was absolutely scary. The skies roared and the earth roared again, daylight fell and darkness fell, lightning flashed, fire blazed, clouds lowered, rained death. Then the splendor vanished, the fire went out, and everything turned to ashes that fell around us. Let's go down the mountain and talk about it, and consider what we should do."

When they came down from the mountain, Gilgamesh took the ax in his hand: he cut down the cedar. When Humbaba heard the noise in the distance he was angry; he cried out: "Who is this that has violated my woods and cut down my cedar?" But the glorious Shamash called them from heaven: "Go ahead, do not be afraid." But now Gilgamesh was overcome with weakness, because sleep had taken him suddenly, a deep sleep restrained him; he lay on the ground, lying silent, as in a dream. When Enkidu touched him he did not rise, when he spoke he did not answer. "O Gilgamesh, Lord of the plain of Kullab, the world is darkening, the shadows have widened upon it, now is the glimmer of twilight. Shamash departed, his shining head extinguished in the womb of his mother Ningal. O Gilgamesh, how long will you lie like this, asleep? Never let the mother who gave birth to you be forced into mourning in the town square."

Finally Gilgamesh heard him; he lies on his breastplate, 'The Voice of the Heroes', weighing thirty shekels; he put it on as if it were a light garment he wore, and covered it completely. He straddled the earth like a bull sniffing the ground and his teeth were clenched. "For the life of my mother Ninsun who gave birth to me, and for the life of my father, the divine Lugulbanda, let me live to be my mother's wonder, as when she nursed me on her lap." A second time he said to him: "For the life of Ninsun my mother who gave birth to me, and for the life of my father, the divine Lugulbanda, until we have fought this man, if he is a man, this god, if he is a god, the road I took to the Land of the Living will not return to the city."

Then Enkidu, the faithful companion, begged, replying: "O my lord, you do not know this monster and that is why you are not afraid. I who know him am terrified. His teeth are dragon fangs, his aspect is like a lion, his charge is the flow of the flood, with his gaze he crushes the trees of the forest and the reeds of the swamp alike. O my Lord, you can go ahead if you choose in this land, but I will go back to the city. I will tell your mother about all your glorious feats until she cries out for joy: and then I will tell her the death that followed until she weeps for her bitterness." But Gilgamesh said: "Immolation and sacrifice are not yet for me, the boat of the dead will not come down, nor will the three-veiled cloth be cut for my shroud. My people will not yet be desolate, nor will the pyre be lit in my house, and my dwelling will be burned in fire. Give me your help today and you will have mine: what can go wrong between us? All living creatures born of flesh will finally sit in the boat of the West, and when it sinks, when the boat of the Magilum sinks, they will be gone; but we'll go ahead and fix our eyes on this monster. If your heart is afraid, throw the fear away; if there is terror in it, it throws terror away. Take your ax in hand and attack. Whoever leaves the struggle unfinished is not at peace."

Humbaba came out of his strong cedar house. Then Enkidu cried out: "O Gilgamesh, remember now your boasting in Uruk. Come on, attack, son of Uruk, there is nothing to fear." When he heard these words his courage raised; he replied: "Hurry up, come near, if the sentry is there don't let him run away into the woods where he will vanish. He has worn the first of his seven splendours but not yet the other six, let's trap him before he is armed." Like a raging wild bull, he sniffed the ground; the guardian of the forest turned full of threats, shouted. Humbaba came from his strong cedar house. He nodded his head and shook it, threatening Gilgamesh; and upon him he fixed his eye, the eye of death. Then Gilgamesh called Shamash and his tears flowed: "O glorious Shamash, I have followed the path you commanded me, but now if you do not send help how can I escape?" The glorious Shamash heard his prayer and summoned the great wind, the north wind, the whirlwind, the storm and the icy wind, the storm and the scorching wind; they came like dragons, like a burning fire, like a serpent that freezes the heart, a devastating flood and the gallows of lightning. The eight winds rose against Humbaba, bumped against his eyes; he was gripped, unable to move forward or backward. Gilgamesh cried out: "For the life of Ninsun my mother and the divine Lugulbanda my father, in the Land of the Living, in this Land I have discovered your abode; my weak arms and small weapons I brought to this land against you, and now I will come into your house."

So he felled the first cedar, cut off its branches and placed them at the foot of the mountain. At the first shot Humbaba ignited, but they continued to advance. They cut down seven cedars, cut and tied the branches and laid them at the foot of the mountain, and seven times Humbaba poured out his glory upon them. When the seventh fire was extinguished, they reached his lair. He patted himself on the thigh with contempt. He approached like a noble wild bull tied to the mountain, a warrior whose elbows are tied together. Tears began in his eyes and he was pale, "Gilgamesh, let me speak. I have never known a mother, no, nor a father who raised me. I was born of the mountain, he raised me, and Enlil appointed me keeper of this forest. Let me go, Gilgamesh, and I will be your servant, you will be my lord; all the trees of the forest that I have tended on the mountain will be yours. I will tear them down and build you a palace." He took him by the hand and led him to his house, so that Gilgamesh's heart was moved with compassion. He swore by heavenly life, by earthly life, by the underworld itself: "O Enkidu, shouldn't the trapped bird return to his nest and the captive man return to his mother's arms?" Enkidu replied: "The strongest of men will fall into fate if he has no judgment. Namtar, the evil fate that knows no distinction between men, will devour him. If the trapped bird returns to its nest, if the captive man returns to her mother's arms, then you my friend will never return to the city where the mother who gave birth to you awaits. He will block the mountain road against you and make the paths impassable."

Humbaba said, "Enkidu, what you said is evil: you, mercenary, dependent for your bread! Out of envy and fear of a rival you uttered bad words." Enkidu said, "Do not listen, Gilgamesh: this Humbaba must die. Kill Humbaba first and then his minions." But Gilgamesh said, "If we touch him, the flame and the glory of the light will be extinguished in confusion, the glory and the charm will vanish, his rays will be extinguished." Enkidu said to Gilgamesh: "He is not like that, my friend. Trap the bird first, and then where will the chicks go? Then we can look for glory and charm, when the chicks run distractedly through the grass."

Gilgamesh listened to the word of his companion, took the ax in his hand, drew the sword from his belt, and struck Humbaba with a sword blow to the neck, and his companion Enkidu struck the second. On the third blow, Humbaba fell. Then followed confusion because this was the guardian of the forest they had cut down to the ground. The cedars trembled for two leagues as Enkidu struck down the guardian of the forest, at whose voice both Hermon and Lebanon trembled. Now the mountains were moved and all the hills, because the guardian of the forest was killed. They attacked the cedars, the seven splendors of Humbaba died out. So they went into the forest carrying the sword of eight talents. They discovered the sacred abodes of the Anunnaki and as Gilgamesh felled the first of the trees of the forest Enkidu cleared their roots to the banks of the Euphrates. They have placed Humbaba before the gods, before Enlil; they kissed the earth and dropped the shroud and laid their heads in front of him. When he saw Humbaba's head, Enlil was angry with them. "Why did you do this? From now on, fire be on your faces, may it eat the bread you eat, may it drink where you drink." Then Enlil took again the flame and the seven splendors which had been of Humbaba: he gave the first to the river, and he gave to the lion, to the stone of execration, to the mountain and to the dreaded daughter of the Queen of Hell.

O Gilgamesh, king and conqueror of the dreadful blaze; wild bull who plunders the mountain, who crosses the sea, glory to him, and from the brave the greater glory is Enki's!

ISHTAR AND GILGAMESH, AND THE DEATH OF ENKIDU

Gilgamesh washed his long locks and cleaned his arms; he threw his hair back from his shoulders; he took off his stained clothes and changed them for new ones. He put on his royal robes and made them fast. When Gilgamesh had donned the crown, the glorious Ishtar looked up at him, seeing the beauty of Gilgamesh. She said: "Come to me Gilgamesh, and be my husband; grant me the seed of your body, let me be your bride and you will be my husband. I will finish for you a chariot of lapis lazuli and gold, with wheels of gold and horns of copper; and you will have mighty storm demons for draft mules. When you enter our home in the fragrance of cedar wood, the threshold and throne will kiss your feet. Kings, rulers and princes will bow down to you; they will bring you tribute from the mountains and the plain. Your sheep will leave twins and your goats triplets; your pack donkey will run faster than the mules; your oxen will be unrivaled and your chariot horses will be famous from afar for their speed."

Gilgamesh opened his mouth and answered the glorious Ishtar: "If I take you as my bride, what gifts can I give in return? What ointments and clothes for your body? I would gladly give you bread and all sorts of food worthy of a god. I'd give you wine worthy of a queen to drink. I would pour barley to fill your barn; but as for making you my wife, I won't. How would it go with me? Your lovers have found you as a brazier that burns in the cold, a back door that keeps out neither gust of wind nor storm, a castle that crushes the garrison, the pitch that blackens the bearer, a water-skin that irritates the bearer, a stone falling from the parapet, a battering ram turned back by the enemy, a sandal that stumbles the wearer. Which of your lovers have you ever loved forever? Which of your pastor have you liked forever? Listen to me as I tell the story of your lovers. There was Tammuz, the lover of your youth, for him you decreed lament, year after year. You loved the roller of a thousand colors, but still you hit him and broke his wing; now in the grove he sits down and shouts: "kappi, kappi, my wing, my wing".

You loved the lion of tremendous strength: you dug graves for him, seven and yet seven again. You have loved the magnificent stallion in battle, and for him you have decreed whip and spur and a snare, to gallop seven leagues by force and to muddy the water before it drinks; and for his mother Silili lamentations. You loved the shepherd of the flock; he baked ash cakes for you day after day, he killed the children for your good. You struck him and turned him into a wolf, now his own little shepherds chase him away, his own hounds afflict his hips. And didn't you love Ishullanu, the gardener of your father's palm grove? He brought you baskets full of endless dates; every day he loaded your table. Then you turned your eyes on him and said, 'Dear Ishullanu, come here to me, let's enjoy your manhood, come on and take me, I'm yours.' Ishullanu replied, 'What are you asking of me? My mother cooked and I ate; why should I come to those like you for contaminated and rotten food? Since when a reed screen was sufficient protection from the frosts?' But when you had heard his answer, you hit him. He has been changed into a blind mole deep in the earth, one whose desire is always beyond his reach. And if you and I were lovers, shouldn't I be served in the same fashion as all these others you once loved?"

When Ishtar heard this she felt very much angry. Her tears poured down in front of her father Anu, and Antum her mother. She said, "Father, Gilgamesh slandered me! He hurled the worst insults at me, he said horrible, unforgivable things!" Anu said to the princess Ishtar, "But might you not have provoked this? Did you try to seduce him? Or did he just start insulting you for no reason at all?"

Ishtar opened her mouth and said again, "My father, please give me the Bull of Heaven to destroy Gilgamesh. I want to bring it to the earth, I want it to kill that liar Gilgamesh and destroy his palace. If you say no, I will smash the gates of the underworld, and a million famished ghouls will ascend to devour the living, and the living will be outnumbered by the dead." Anusa said to great Ishtar, "If I do what you desire there will be seven years of drought throughout Uruk when grains will be seedless husks. Have you saved grain enough for the people and grass for the cattle? Ishtar replied. "I have saved grain for the people, grass for the cattle; for seven years of seedless husks' there is grain and there is grass enough."

When Anu heard what Ishtar had said he gave her the Bull of Heaven to lead by the halter down to Uruk: When they reached the gates of

Uruk the Bull went to the river; with his first snort cracks opened in the earth and, a hundred warriors fell down to death. With his second snort cracks opened and two hundred fell in and died. With his third snort cracks opened, Enkidu fell in, but quickly recovered, he dodged aside and leapt on the Bull and grabbed its horns. The Bull of Heaven foamed in its face, it brushed him with its thick tail. Enkidu shouted to Gilgamesh, "My friend, we bragged that we would leave eternal names behind us. Now stick your sword between the shoulders and the horns." So Gilgamesh followed the Bull, he seized the thick of its tail, he thrust the sword between the shoulder and the horns and slew the Bull. When they had killed the Bull of Heaven they ripped out its heart and offered it to Shamash, then they both bowed before him and sat down like brothers.

Ishtar rose on tiptoe and climbed the great wall of Uruk; jumped up on the tower and uttered a curse "Woe to Gilgamesh, not only did he slander me-now the brute has killed his own punishment, the Bull of Heaven." When Enkidu heard these words he tore up the Bull's right thigh and threw it in her face saying, "If only I could catch you, this is what I would do to you, I would rip you apart and drape the Bull's guts over your arms!" Then Ishtar called together her people, the dancing and singing girls, the prostitutes of the temple, the courtesans. Over the thigh of the Bull of Heaven she began a solemn lamentation.

Gilgamesh called the blacksmiths and the armorers, all together. They admired the immensity of the horns. They were plated with two-finger-thick lapis lazuli. They were thirty pounds each in weight, and their capacity in oil was six measures, which he gave to his guardian god, Lugulbanda. But he took the horns into the palace and hung them up the wall. Then they washed their hands in the Euphrates, embraced and left. They drove through the streets of Uruk where the heroes had gathered to see them, and Gilgamesh called the singing girls: "Who is more glorious of heroes, who is the most eminent among men?" "Gilgamesh is the most glorious of heroes, Gilgamesh is the most eminent among men." And now there were banquets, celebrations and rejoicing in the palace, until the heroes lay down saying: "Now we will rest for the night."

When daylight came, Enkidu stood up and said to Gilgamesh, "O my brother, such a dream I had tonight." Anu, Enlil, Ea and the heavenly Shamash consulted, and Anu said to Enlil: "Because they killed the Bull of Heaven and because they killed Humbaba who protected the Cedar Mountain, one of them must die." Then the glorious Shamash replied to the hero Enlil: "Was it at your command that they killed the Bull of Heaven and killed Humbaba, so that Enkidu must die innocent?" Enlil hurled himself furiously in front of the glorious Shamash: "You dare say this, you who walked around with them every day as one of them!"

Thus Enkidu lay stretched out before Gilgamesh; his tears flowed from him and he said to Gilgamesh: "O my brother, as dear as you are to me, brother, yet they will take me from you." Then he said: "I must sit on the threshold of the dead and never again will I see my dear brother with my own eyes."

As Enkidu lay alone in his sickness, he cursed the door as if it were living flesh, "You there, door wood, dull and numb, foolish, I searched for you for over twenty leagues until I saw the towering cedar. There is no wood like you in our land. Seventy-two cubits in height and twenty-four in width, the pin and the ferrule and the jambs are perfect. A master craftsman from Nippur created you; but oh, if I had known the conclusion! If I had known this was all the good that would come of it, I would have raised the ax and torn you apart and placed a wattle gate here instead. Ah, if only some future king brought you here, or some god fashioned you. Let him erase my name and write his, and the curse be upon him instead of Enkidu."

With the first light of dawn Enkidu raised his head and wept before the Sun God, in the splendor of the sunlight his tears flowed down. "Sun God, I beg you, regarding that vile trapper, that hunter of nothing because of which I had to catch less than my companion; let him catch less, make his game meager, make him limp, taking the smallest of every share, let his prey escape his nets."

When he had cursed the trapper at will, he turned to the harlot. He cursed her too. "As for you, woman, with a great curse I curse you! I promise you a destiny for eternity. My curse will come upon you soon and suddenly. You will have no place for your businesses, because you will not stay at home with other girls in the tavern, but you will do your business in places contaminated by the drunkard's vomit. Your wages will be potter's land, your thieves will be thrown into the hovel, you will sit at the crossroads in the dust of the potter's quarter, at night you will make your bed in the dunghill and during the day you will stand in the shadow of the wall. Prickly shrubs and thorns will tear your feet, the drunk and the dry will hit your cheek and your mouth will ache. Let yourself strip of your purple dyes, because I too once with my wife in the wilderness I had all the treasure I wanted."

When Shamash heard Enkidu's words, he called him from heaven: "Enkidu, why do you curse the woman, the lover who taught you to eat bread worthy of the gods and drink the wine of kings? Did not she who clothed you in a magnificent robe give you glorious Gilgamesh for your mate, and Gilgamesh, your brother, made you rest on a royal bed and lie down on a couch to his left? He made the princes of the earth kiss your feet, and now all the people of Uruk are weeping and crying for you. When you are dead he will grow his hair for you, he will wear a lion skin and wander the desert."

When Enkidu heard the glorious Shamash, his angry heart calmed down, he withdrew the curse and said, "Woman, I promise you another fate. The mouth that cursed you will bless you! Kings, princes and nobles will adore you. Because of you a man even if twelve miles away will clap his hand on his thigh and his hair will twitch. For you he will unfasten his belt and open his treasure and you will have your desire for him; lapis lazuli, gold and carnelian from the heap in the treasury. A ring for your hand and a robe will be yours. The priest will lead you into the presence of the gods. Because of you, a wife, a mother of seven children, was abandoned."

Enkidu's innards were churning, lying there alone, with bitterness of spirit he opened his heart to his friend. "I was the one who felled the cedar, I was the one who cleared the forest, I who killed Humbaba and now I see what became of me. Listen, my friend, this is the dream I had tonight. The heavens roared, and the earth thundered an answer; among them I was faced with a terrible being, the dark-faced bird-man; his face resembled a leech, his foot was a lion's foot, his hand was an eagle's claw. He fell on me and his claws were in my hair, he held me tight and I choked; then he transformed me so that my arms became feather-covered wings. He turned his gaze towards me, and led me to the palace of Irkalla, the Queen of Darkness, to the house from which no one who enters returns, along the road from which there is no return.

There is the house whose people sit in the dark; dust is their food and clay their flesh. They are dressed like birds with wings to cover themselves, they do not see the light, they dwell in darkness. I entered the house of dust and I saw the kings of the earth, their crowns laid forever; leaders and princes, all who once wore royal crowns and ruled the world in the old days. Those who had stood in the place of gods like Ann and Enlil now stood as servants to take cooked meat to the dust house, to bring cooked meat and cold water from the water-skin. In the house of dust into which I entered were high priests and acolytes, priests of magic spell and ecstasy; there were temple servants, and there was Etana, that king of Dish whom the eagle carried to heaven. I also saw Samuqan, god of cattle, and there was Ereshkigal, the Queen of the Underworld, and Befit-Sheri crouched down before her, she who is the archivist of the gods and holds the book of death. She was reading. She raised her head, saw me and spoke: 'Who has brought him here?' Then I woke up like a bled man wandering alone in an expanse of rashes; like one the bailiff has kidnapped and his heart beats with terror."

Gilgamesh had taken off his clothes, listened to his words and wept quick tears, Gilgamesh listened and his tears flowed. He spoke to Enkidu: "Who is there in strong-walled Uruk who has wisdom like this? Strange things have been said, why does your heart speak so strange? The dream was wonderful but the terror was great; we must treasure the dream whatever the terror; because the dream showed that misery finally reaches the healthy man, the end of life is pain." And Gilgamesh complained, "Now I will pray to the great gods, because my friend had a disturbing dream."

The day when Enkidu had dreamed ended and he was struck by an illness. One whole day he lay on the bed and his suffering increased. He said to Gilgamesh, the friend for whom he had left the wilderness, "Once I ran for you, for the water that gives life, and now I have nothing left." A second day he lay down on the bed and Gilgamesh watched over him, but the sickness increased. A third day he lay down on his bed, called Gilgamesh, waking him up. Now he was weak and his eyes were blind with tears. Ten days he laid and his sufferings increased, eleven and twelve days he laid on his bed of pain. Then he called Gilgamesh: "My friend, the great goddess has cursed me and I must die in shame. I will not die like a man who has fallen in battle; I was afraid of falling, but happy is the man who falls in battle, because I must die in shame." And Gilgamesh wept for Enkidu. At the crack of dawn he raised his voice and said to the counselors of Uruk:

"Hear me, great ones of Uruk,

I cry for Enkidu, my friend.
Moaning bitterly like a grieving woman I cry for my brother.
O Enkidu, my brother,
You were the ax by my side,
The strength of my hand, the sword in my belt,
The shield in front of me,
A glorious robe, my most beautiful ornament;
An evil fate has robbed me.
The wild ass and the gazelle they were father and mother,
All the long-tailed creatures that fed you Cry for you
All the wild things of the plain and pastures;
The paths you loved in the cedar forest Day and night murmur.
Let the great ones of the strong walled Uruk Cry for you;
Let the finger bless Be stretched in mourning;
Enkidu, younger brother. Listen,
There is an echo throughout the country Like a grieving mother.
Weep all the paths where we have walked together;
And the beasts we hunted, the bear and the hyena,
Tiger and panther, leopard and lion,
The deer and the ibex, the bull and the doe.
The river along whose banks we walked,
cries for you,
Ula of Elam and dear Euphrates
Where once we drew water for water-skins.
The mountain we climbed where we killed the watchman,
He cries for you.
The warriors of Uruk with strong walls where the Bull of Heaven
was killed,
Cry for you.
All the people of Eridu Weep for you Enkidu.
Those who brought grain for your food Cry for you now;
Who smeared oil on your back Cry for you now;
Who poured the beer for you I cry for you now.
The harlot who anointed you with a perfumed ointment She com-
plains for you now;
The women of the palace, who brought you a wife,
A chosen ring of good advice,
I moan for you now.

And your young brothers As if they were women Go with long hair in mourning.

What is this sleep holding you back now?

You are lost in the dark and you cannot hear me.';

He touched his heart but it did not beat, nor did he open his eyes again. So Gilgamesh spread a veil, as for a bride, over his friend. He began to rage like a lion, like a lioness robbed of her young. He paced around the bed, tore out his hair and scattered it around. He dragged off his beautiful robes and threw them down as if they were his abominations.

At the first light of dawn Gilgamesh cried out, "I made you rest on a royal bed, you laid down on a bed on my left, the princes of the earth kissed your feet. I will make all the people of Uruk weep over you and raise the dirge of the dead. The joyful people will humble themselves with pain; and when you return to dust, I will make my hair grow for your sake, I will wander the desert under the skin of a lion." Even the next day, in the first light, Gilgamesh complained; seven days and seven nights he wept for Enkidu, until the worms fastened. Only then did he give him back to the earth, because the Anunnaki, the judges, had taken it.

Then Gilgamesh issued a proclamation for the country, summoned all the coppersmiths, goldsmiths and stonemasons and commanded them: "Make a statue of my friend." The statue was modeled with a large weight of lapis lazuli for the breast and gold for the body. A hardwood table was set and above it a carnelian bowl full of honey and a lapis lazuli bowl full of butter. These were offered to the Sun; and crying he left.

THE SEARCH FOR EVERLASTING LIFE

Gilgamesh wept bitterly for his friend Enkidu; he wandered the desert like a hunter, wandered the plains; in his bitterness he cried: "How can I rest, how can I be at peace? Despair is in my heart. What my brother is now, that will be me when I am dead. Since I am afraid of death, I will do as best I can to find Utnapishtim, the one called the Faraway, because he has entered the assembly of the gods." So Gilgamesh traveled in the wilderness, wandered the prairies, a long journey, in search of Utnapishtim, whom the gods took after the great flood; and they put him to live in the land of Dilmun, in the garden of the sun; and to him alone, among men, gave eternal life.

At night, when he came to the mountain passes, Gilgamesh prayed: "In these mountain passes long ago I saw lions, I was afraid and raised my eyes to the moon; I prayed and my prayers went to the gods, so now, oh moon god Sin, protect me." When he had prayed he laid down to sleep, until he was awakened from a dream. He saw the lions around him glorying in life; then he took his ax in his hand, drew the sword from his belt and fell upon them like an arrow from the rope, and struck them, destroyed them and scattered them.

So finally Gilgamesh came to Mashu, the great mountains of which he had heard many things, which guard the rising and setting of the sun. His twin peaks are as high as the wall of heaven and its paps descend to the underworld. The Scorpions guard its gate, half man and half dragon; their glory is terrifying, their gaze strikes death in men, their sparkling halo sweeps the mountains that guard the rising sun. When Gilgamesh saw them, he only covered his eyes for a moment; then he took courage and approached. When they saw him so undeterred the Scorpio-Man called his companion: "He who comes to us now is the flesh of the gods." The companion of the Scorpio-man replied: "Two thirds is god, but one third is man."

Then he called the man Gilgamesh, called the son of the gods: "Why did you make such a great journey? What have you traveled for thus far, crossing dangerous waters; tell me the reason for your coming."

Gilgamesh replied, "For Enkidu; I loved him dearly, together we have endured all kinds of difficulties; I have come because of him, because the common lot of man has taken him. I cried for him day and night, I would not give up his body for burial, I thought my friend would come back because of my crying. Since he's gone, my life is nothing; that is why I traveled here in search of my father Utnapishtim; for men say that he entered the assembly of the gods and found eternal life: I wish to ask him about the living and the dead." The Scorpio-Man opened his mouth and said, speaking to Gilgamesh, "No man born of woman has done what you say, no mortal man has gone to the mountain; his length is twelve leagues of darkness; there is no light in it, but the heart is oppressed by darkness. From sunrise to sunset there is no light." Gilgamesh said, "Even though I should go with sorrow and pain, with sighs and with tears, yet I must go. Open the door of the mountain." And the Scorpio-Man said, "Go, Gilgamesh, I allow you to pass through the mountain of Mashu and through the high ranges; may your feet carry you home safely. The door to the mountain is open."

When Gilgamesh heard this, he did as the Scorpio-Man had said, followed the path of the sun to its rise through the mountain. When he had made a league, the darkness thickened around him, because there was no light, he could see nothing ahead and nothing behind him. After two leagues the darkness was thick and there was no light, he could see nothing ahead and nothing behind him. After three leagues the darkness was thick, and there was no light, he could see nothing ahead and nothing behind him. After four leagues the darkness was thick and there was no light, he could see nothing ahead and nothing behind him. At the end of five leagues the darkness was thick and there was no light, he could see nothing ahead and nothing behind him. At the end of six leagues the darkness was thick and there was no light, he could see nothing ahead and nothing behind him. When he had made seven leagues the darkness was thick and there was no light, he could see nothing ahead and nothing behind him. When he had gone eight leagues, Gilgamesh let out a great cry, because the darkness was thick and he could see nothing ahead and nothing behind him. After nine leagues he felt the north-wind in his face, but the darkness was thick and there was no light, he could see nothing ahead and nothing behind him. After ten leagues the end was near: after eleven leagues the light of dawn appeared. At the end of twelve leagues the sun came out.

There was the garden of the gods; all around him were bushes bearing buds. Seeing it immediately he got out, because there was a carnelian fruit with the vine hanging from it, beautiful to look at; Lapis Lazuli leaves hanging thick with fruit, sweet to see. For thorns and thistles there were hematite and rare stones, agate and sea pearls. As Gilgamesh strolled in the garden by the sea Shamash saw him, and saw that he was dressed with the skin of animals and he had eaten their flesh. He was distressed, and he spoke and said, "No mortal man has ever followed this path before, nor will he, as long as the winds carry the sea." And to Gilgamesh he said, "You will never find the life you are looking for." Gilgamesh said to the glorious Shamash, "Now that I have toiled and wandered so far into the wilderness, must I sleep and let the earth cover my head forever? Let my eyes see the sun until they are dazzled by the gaze. Even if I am no better than a dead man, let me still see the sunlight."

Beside the sea lives the woman of the vine, the creator of wine; Siduri sits in the garden by the sea, with the golden bowl and the golden vats that her gods have given her. She is covered with a veil; and where she sits she sees Gilgamesh coming towards her, dressed in skins, the flesh of the gods in his body, but despair in his heart, and his face like the face of one who made a long journey. She looked, and as she peered into the distance she said in her very heart, "Surely this is a criminal; where is he going now?" And she barred the gate with the crossbar and fired the latch at the house. But Gilgamesh, hearing the sound of the bolt, raised his head and put his foot in the door; he called her: "Young woman, who makes wine, why do you close your door?" What did you see that made you bar the gate? I will break your door and break into your door, because I am Gilgamesh who took and killed the Bull of Heaven, I killed the guardian of the cedar forest, I overthrew Humbaba who lived in the forest and I killed the lions in the mountain pass."

Then Siduri said to him, "If you are that Gilgamesh who took and killed the Bull of Heaven, who killed the guardian of the cedar forest, who destroyed Humbaba who dwelt in the forest and killed the lions on the mountain passes, for your cheeks are so hungry and why is your face so drawn? Why despair in your heart and your face like the face of someone who has traveled a long way? Yes, why your face is burned with heat and cold, and why do you come here to wander the pastures in search of the wind?"

Gilgamesh replied, "And why shouldn't my cheeks be hungry and my face drawn? Despair is in my heart and my face is the face of someone who has made a long journey, has been burned by heat and cold. Why shouldn't I wander the pastures looking for the wind? My friend, my younger brother, the one who hunted the wild ass of the desert and the panther of the plains, my younger brother who captured and killed the Bull of Heaven and overthrew Humbaba in the cedar forest, my friend who was very dear to me and who endured the dangers beside me, Enkidu my brother, whom I adored, the end of mortality has reached him. I wept for him seven days and seven nights until the worm fastened on him. Because of my brother I am afraid of death, because of my brother I wander in the wilderness and I cannot rest. But now, young woman who makes wine, since I have seen your face, do not let me see the face of death that I fear so much."

She replied, "Gilgamesh, where are you running? You will never find that life you are looking for. When the gods created man, they gave him death, but kept life in their custody. As for you, Gilgamesh, fill your belly with good things; day and night, night and day, dance and have fun, celebrate and rejoice. Let your clothes be fresh, bathe in the water, take care of the child who holds your hand and make your wife happy in your embrace; because this is also the destiny of man."

But Gilgamesh said to Siduri, the young woman, "How can I be silent, how can I rest, when Enkidu whom I love is dust, and I too will die and be buried. You live by the sea and look into its heart; young woman, tell me now, what is the way to Utnapishtim, the son of Ubara-Tutu? What are the indications for the passage; give me, oh, give me directions. I will cross the ocean if it is possible; if it isn't, I'll go even farther into the wilderness." The winemaker said to him, "Gilgamesh, one does not cross the ocean; who has come, since ancient times, has not been able to cross that sea. The Sun in its glory crosses the ocean, but who besides Shamash has ever crossed it? The place and the passage are difficult, and deep are the waters of death that flow in between. Gilgamesh, how will you cross the ocean? When you get to the waters of death what will you do? But Gilgamesh, down in the woods you will find Urshanabi, the ferryman of Utnapishtim; with him are holy things, things of stone. He is modeling the snake bow of the boat. Look at him well, and if it is possible, maybe you will cross the waters with him; but if that's not possible, then you have to go back."

When Gilgamesh heard this, he was angry. He took his ax in his hand, and his dagger from his belt. He crawled forward and fell on them like a javelin. Then he went into the forest and sat down. Urshanabi saw the dagger flash and heard the ax, and banged his head, as Gilgamesh had shattered the boat's rig in his anger. Urshanabi said to him, "Tell me, what's your name? I am Urshanabi, the ferryman of Utnapishtim the Faraway." He replied: "Gilgamesh is my name, I come from Uruk, from the house of Anu." Then Urshanabi said to him, "Why are your cheeks so hungry and your face drawn? Because the despair in your heart and your face like the face of someone who has made a long journey; yes, why your face is burned with heat and cold, and why do you come here to wander the pastures in search of the wind?"

Gilgamesh said to him, "Why shouldn't my cheeks be hungry and my face drawn? Despair is in my heart, and my face is the face of someone who has traveled a long way. I was burned by the heat and the cold. Why shouldn't I wander the pastures? My friend, my younger brother who took and killed the Bull of Heaven and overthrew Humbaba in the cedar forest, my friend who was very dear to me and who endured dangers beside me, Enkidu my brother whom I loved, the end of mortality has reached him. I wept for him seven days and seven nights until the worm fastened on him. Because of my brother I am afraid of death, because of my brother I wander in the wilderness. His fate weighs on me. How can I be silent, how can I rest? He is dust and I too will die and be buried forever. I am afraid of death, so Urshanabi, tell me what is the way to Utnapishtim? If possible I will cross the waters of death; otherwise I will wander even farther across the wilderness."

Urshanabi said to him, "Gilgamesh, your own hands have prevented you from crossing the ocean; when you destroyed the boat's equipment you destroyed its safety." Then the two talked about it and Gilgamesh said, "Why are you so angry with me, Urshanabi, because you yourself cross the sea day and night, in all seasons you cross it" "Gilgamesh, those things you have destroyed, their property is to take me to the water, to prevent the waters of death from touching me. That is why I have kept them, but you have destroyed them, and the urn meanders with them. But now, Gilgamesh, go to the forest; with your ax cut one hundred and twenty poles, cut them sixty cubits long, paint them with bitumen, put ferrules on them and bring them back."

Heard this, Gilgamesh went into the forest, cut down one hundred and twenty poles; he cut them sixty cubits long, painted them with bitumen, placed ferrules on them and took them to Urshanabi. Then they got on the boat, Gilgamesh and Urshanabi together, throwing it on the ocean waves. For three days they ran as if it were a one month and fifteen day voyage, and finally Urshanabi took the boat to the waters of death. Then Urshanabi said to Gilgamesh, "Come on, take a pole and stick it in, but don't let your hands touch the water. Gilgamesh, take a second pole, take a third, take a fourth pole. Now, Gilgamesh, take a fifth, take a sixth and a seventh pole. Gilgamesh, take an eighth, and ninth, a tenth pole. Gilgamesh, take an eleventh pole, take a twelfth pole." After a hundred and twenty pushes Gilgamesh had used the last pole. Then he removed his clothes, used his arms for a mast and its cover for a sail. So Urshanabi the ferryman brought Gilgamesh to Utnapishtim, which they call the Faraway, who lives in Dihnun in the place of transit of the Sun, east of the mountain. To him only among men the gods had given eternal life.

Now Utnapishtim, where he lay at ease, looked into the distance and said in his heart, pondering to himself: "Why the boat sails here without a tackle and without a mast; why are the sacred stones destroyed, and why does the master not sail the boat? That man who comes is not mine; where I look I see a man whose body is covered with animal skins. Who is this that goes up the shore behind Urshanabi, because he is surely not my man?" So Utnapishtim looked at him and he said, "What is your name, you who come here wearing beast skins, with hungry cheeks and a drawn face? Where are you running now? Why did you make this great journey, crossing the seas whose passage is hard? Tell me the reason for your coming."

He replied: "Gilgamesh is my name. I come from Uruk, from the house of Anu." Then Utnapishtim said to him, "If you are Gilgamesh, why are your cheeks so hungry and your face drawn? Why is despair in your heart and your face like the face of who has made a long journey? Yes, because your face is burned with heat and cold; and why do you come here, wandering in the wilderness in search of the wind?"

Gilgamesh said to him, "Why shouldn't my cheeks be hungry and my face drawn? Despair is in my heart and mine face is the face of one who has made a long journey. He was burned with heat and cold. Why shouldn't I ramble? the pastures? My friend, my younger brother who kidnapped and killed the Bull of Heaven and overthrew Humbaba in the cedar forest, my friend who was very dear to me and who endured dangers next to me, Enkidu, my brother I loved, the the end of mortality has reached him. I wept for him seven days and seven nights until the worm attached itself to him. because of me brother I'm afraid of death; because of my brother I wander around the desert. His fate weighs on me. How can I shut up, how can I rest? He is dust and I too will die and be laid in the earth forever." Again Gilgamesh said, speaking to Utnapishtim, "It is to see Utnapishtim that we call the Faraway that I have made this journey. For this I have wandered the world, I have crossed many difficult mountains, I have crossed the seas, I have grown tired of travelling; my joints ache and I have not slept which is sweet. My clothes were worn out before I came to Siduri's house. I killed the bear and the hyena, the lion and the panther, the tiger, the deer and the ibex, all game species and small pasture creatures. I ate their flesh and put on their skins; and that's how I got there at the door of the young woman, the winemaker, who barred her door of pitch and bitumen against me. But from her I had information about the trip; so then I went to Urshanabi, the ferryman, and with him I crossed the waters of death. Oh, Utnapishtim, you who have entered the assembly of the gods, I wish to ask you about the living and the dead, how will I find the life I'm looking for?"

Utnapishtim said: "There is no permanence. Do we build a house that will last forever, do we seal a contract to keep? Always? The brothers share an inheritance to keep forever, does it last the time of the floods of the rivers? She is just the nymph of the dragonfly that strips the larva and sees the Sun in her glory. From ancient times there is no permanence. The sleeping and the dead, how similar they are, are like a painted death. What is between the master and the servant when they both have fulfilled their destiny? When the Anunnaki, the judges, gather and Mammetun the mother of destinies, together they decree the destinies of men. Life and death assign but do not reveal the day of death."

Then Gilgamesh said to Utnapishtim the Faraway, "Now I look at you, Utnapishtim, and your appearance is not different from mine; there is nothing strange about your characteristics. I thought I should find you like a hero prepared for battle, but you're here relaxing on your back. Tell me really, why did you come to enter the company of the gods and to possess eternal life?" Utnapishtim said to Gilgamesh,

"I will reveal to you a mystery, I will reveal to you a secret of the gods."

THE STORY OF THE FLOOD

"Do you know the city Shurrupak, located on the banks of the Euphrates? That city became old and the gods that were in it were old. There was Anu, lord of the firmament, their father, and the warrior Enlil their adviser, Ninurta the adjutant and Ennugi guardian of the canals; and with them was Ea too. In those days the world swarmed, people multiplied, the world bellowed like a wild bull, and the great god was aroused by the clamor. Enlil heard the clamor and said to the gods in council, 'The tumult of humanity is intolerable and sleep is no longer possible because of Babel.' So the gods agreed to exterminate humanity. Enlil did this, but Ea because of his oath warned me in a dream. He whispered their words to my reed house, 'Reed house, reed house! Wall, o wall, hear reed house, reflect on the wall; O man of Shurrupak, son of Ubara-Tutu; demolish your house and build a boat, abandon your possessions and seek life, despise earthly goods and save your soul alive. Tear down your house, I say, and build a boat. These are the measures of the boat as you will build it: let hex beam equal her length, its bridge is covered as the vault that covers the abyss; then take on the boat the seed of all living creatures.'

When I had understood I said to my lord,

'Behold, what you have commanded I will honor and execute, but how will I answer the people, the city, the elderly?' Then Ea said to me, his servant, 'Tell them this: I have learned that Enlil is angry with me, I no longer dare to enter his land nor dwell in the city; I will go down to the Gulf to live with Ea my lord. But on you he will rain down abundance, rare fish and shy wild birds, a rich tide of the harvest. In the evening the knight of the storm he will bring you grain in torrents.'

At the first light of dawn my whole family gathered around me, the children brought pitch and men all that was needed. On the fifth day I laid the keel and the ribs, then stared at the planking. The ground space was one acre, each side of the bridge measured one hundred and twenty cubits, forming a square. I built six bridges below, seven in all, I divided them into nine sections with bulkheads in between. I drove in wedges where needed, saw the punt poles and deposited the supplies. The porters carried the oil in the baskets, I poured the pitch into the furnace and asphalt and oil; the more oil was consumed in the caulking, the more the owner of the boat took into his provisions. I slaughtered oxen for the people and I killed sheep every day. I gave the shipwrights to drink wine as if it were river water, raw wine and red wine and oil and white wine. There was feasting then as there is at the time of the New Year's festivity; I myself have anointed my head. On the seventh day the boat was complete.

Then the launch was full of difficulties; there was displacement of ballast up and down until two thirds were submerged. I loaded it with all that I had of gold and living things, my family, my relatives, the beast of the fields both wild and tame, and all the craftsmen. I sent them aboard, because the time Shamash had ordered was already up when he said, 'In the evening, when the storm rider will bring down the destructive rain, board the boat and fasten it.' The time was up, evening came, the rider of the storm brought down the rain. I looked at the weather and it was terrible, so I too went aboard the boat and battened it down. Everything was now complete, the splinting and caulking; so I entrusted the helm to Puzur-Amurri the helmsman, with the navigation and care of the whole boat.

At the first light of dawn a black cloud came from the horizon; thundered from inside where Adad, the lord of the storm, was riding. In front of the hill and plain Shullat and Hanish, heralds of the storm, drove. Then the gods of the abyss arose; Nergal tore up the dikes of the shallows, Ninurta the warlord tore down the dikes, and the seven judges of hell, the Annunaki, raised their torches, illuminating the earth with their livid flame. An astonishment of despair rose to heaven as the storm god turned daylight into darkness as he smashed the earth like a cup. A whole day the storm raged, gathering fury as it went, pouring over the people like the tides of battle; an imam could not see his brother, nor could people be seen from heaven. Even the gods were terrified by the flood, they fled into the highest heaven, the firmament of Anna; they crouched against the walls, huddled like idiots. Then Ishtar, the sweet-voiced Queen of Heaven, cried out like a woman in labor: 'Alas, the old days are reduced to dust because I have commanded evil; why have I thus commanded evil in the council of all gods? Wars destroy the people, but are they not my people, why

have I begotten them? Now, like fish offspring, they float in the ocean.'
The great gods of heaven and hell wept, covered their mouths.

For six days and six nights the winds blew, torrent and storm and
flood engulfed the world, storm and flood raged together like armies at
war. At dawn on the seventh day, the storm from the south subsided, the
sea subsided, the flood subsided; I looked at the face of the world and
there was silence, all humanity was transformed to clay. The surface of
the sea laid flat like a roof; I opened a hatch and the light fell on my face.
Then I bowed deeply, sat down and cried, tears streaming down my
face, because the destruction brought by the water was everywhere. In
vain I sought land, but fourteen leagues distant a mountain appeared,
and there the boat ran aground; on Mount Nisir the boat held steady,
held steady, and did not move. One day it resisted, and a second day on
Nisir's mountain it resisted and did not move. A third day and a fourth
day it stood still on the mountain and did not move; a fifth day and a
sixth day it stood still on the mountain. At dawn on the seventh day I
freed a dove and let it go. She flew away, but finding no resting place
she returned. Then I untied a swallow, and she flew away but finding
no resting place she returned. I freed a raven, she saw that the waters
had receded, she ate, she flew, she caw and did not return. Then I threw
everything open on the roof, I did a sacrifice and made a libation on the
top of the mountain. Seven and seven more cauldrons I erected on
their supports, I heaped wood and rush and cedar and myrtle. When
the gods smelled the sweet taste, they gathered like flies on the sacrifice.
Then, finally, Ishtar also came, raised her necklace with the jewels of
the sky that once Anu had given her to please her. 'O you gods present
here, for the lapis lazuli around my neck I will remember these days as
I remember the jewels of my throat; these last days I will not forget
them. All the gods gather around the sacrifice, except Enlil. He do not
come near this offering, because without thinking he brought the flood;
he handed my people over to destruction.'

When Enlil arrived, when he saw the boat, he was furious and puffed
up with rage against the gods, the army of heaven, 'Have any of these
mortals escaped? None would have survived the destruction.' Then
the god of wells and canals Ninurta said to the warrior Enlil: 'Who is
there of the gods who can devise without Ea? Is Ea only that knows all
things.' Then Ea spoke to the warrior Enlil, 'The wisest of the gods, the
hero Enlil, how could you so foolishly bring down the flood?

Put his sin on the sinner,
Put his transgression on the wrongdoer,
Punish him a little when he goes wild,
Don't push it too hard or it will perish,
What if a lion devastated humanity? Rather than the flood,
What if a wolf devastated humanity? Rather than the flood,
What if that famine had ruined the world? Rather than the flood,
What if that pestilence had wasted humanity? Rather than the flood.
It was not I who revealed the secret of the gods; the sage learned this
in a dream. Now listen to your advice what will be done with him.'

Then Enlil got into the boat, took my wife and me by the hand
and made us get into the boat and kneel on either side, he standing
between us. He touched our foreheads to bless us saying, 'In the past
Utnapishtim was a mortal man; henceforth he and his wife will live in
the distance at the mouth of rivers.' So the gods took me and put me
here to live in the distance, at the mouth of the rivers."

THE RETURN

– Utnapishtim said, "As for you, Gilgamesh, who will gather the gods for your sake, so that you may find the life that you are looking for? But if you wish, come and test yourself: prevail over sleep for six days and seven nights." But as Gilgamesh sat there resting on his heels, a haze of sleep like soft wool torn from fleece slipped on him, and Utnapishtim said to his wife, "Look at him now, the strong man who would like eternal life, even now the mists of sleep envelop him." His wife replied to him, "Touch the man to wake him up, so that he can return to his own land in peace, returning by the door by which he had come." Utnapishtim said to his wife, "All men are deceivers, you too will try to deceive; So bake some loaves, a loaf every day, and place it next to his head; and mark the wall to count the days he slept."

So she baked some loaves, a loaf every day, and put it next to his head, and marked on the wall the days he slept; and a day came when the first loaf was hard, the second was like leather, the third was soggy, the crust of the fourth was moldy, the fifth was moldy, the sixth was fresh, and the seventh was still on the coals. Then Utnapishtim touched him and he woke up. Gilgamesh said to Utnapishtim the Faraway, "I barely slept when you touched me and woke me up." But Utnapishtim said, "Count these loaves and learn how many days you slept, because your first is hard, your second is like leather, your third is mushy, your fourth's crust is moldy, your fifth is moldy, your sixth is fresh and your seventh was still above the glowing coals when I touched you and woke you up. Gilgamesh said, "What must I do, O Utnapishtim, where will I go? Already the thief in the night has taken my limbs, death inhabits my room; everywhere mine foot rests, there I find death."

Then Utnapishtim spoke to Urshanabi the ferryman: "Woe to you Urshanabi, now and forever you have become hateful to this port; it is not for you, nor for you are the crossings of this sea. Go now, banished from the shore. But this man you walked before, bringing him here, whose body is covered with filth and whose limbs have been ruined by wild skins, take him to the washroom. There he will wash his long hair clean like snow in water, tear off the skin and let the sea take them away, and the beauty of his body will be shown, the fillet on his forehead will be renewed and receive clothes to cover his nakedness. Until he reaches his own city and his journey is accomplished, these clothes will show no signs of age, they will wear like a new suit." So Urshanabi took Gilgamesh and led him to the wash house, washed his long hair clean as snow in water, threw off his skins, which the sea was taking away, and showed the beauty of his body. He renewed the fillet on his forehead, and to cover his nakedness gave him clothes that would show no signs of age, but would wear like a new garment until he reached his own city, and his journey was accomplished.

Then Gilgamesh and Urshanabi threw the boat over the water and went aboard, and prepared to set sail; but the wife of Utnapishtim the Faraway said to him: "Gilgamesh has come here tired, he is tired; what will you give him to bring him back to his country?" Thus spoke Utnapishtim, and Gilgamesh took a pole and carried the boat ashore. "Gilgamesh, you came here as a weary man, you got worn out; what do I give you to bring? Do you go back to your country? Gilgamesh, I will reveal to you a secret thing, it is a mystery of the gods what I am telling you. There is a plant that grows under water, it has a sting like a thorn, like a rose; it will hurt your hands, but if you can catch it, then your hands will hold what gives man back his lost youth."

When Gilgamesh heard this, he opened the locks for a gentle current of water to carry him into the deepest channel; tied heavy stones to his feet to be dragged down into the water bed. There he saw the plant grow; though it stung him he took it in his hands; then he cut the heavy stones off his feet, and the sea carried him and threw him ashore. Gilgamesh said to Urshanabi the ferryman: "Come here and see this wonderful plant. By virtue of his virtue a man can regain all his former strength. I will take it to the strong-walled Uruk; there I will feed it to the old men. Its name will be 'The old men are young again'; and eventually I'll eat it myself and get all my lost youth back." So Gilgamesh returned by the door through which he had passed, Gilgamesh and Ursanabi went together. They walked their twenty leagues and then broke their fast; after thirty leagues they stopped for the night.

Gilgamesh saw a well of fresh water and went down to bathe; but at the bottom of the pond lay a snake, and the snake felt the sweetness of the flower. It got out of the water and tore it off, and immediately shed its skin and went back to the well. Then Gilgamesh sat down and wept, tears running down his face, and took Urshanabi's hand; "O Urshanabi, was that why I struggled with my hands, was that why I tore out my heart's blood? For me I have not earned anything; not me, but the beast of the earth enjoys it now. Already the stream brought it back twenty leagues to the canals where I found it. I found a sign and now I have lost it. Let's leave the boat on the shore and go."

After twenty leagues they broke their fast, after thirty leagues they stopped for the night; in three days they had made a journey of one month and fifteen days. When the journey was complete, they arrived at Umk, the fortified city. Gilgamesh spoke to him, to Urshanabi the ferryman, "Urshanabi, climb the wall of Umk, inspect its foundation terrace and examine the brickwork well; see if it is not made of baked bricks; and did the seven wise men not lay these foundations? A third of the whole is a city, a third is a garden and a third is a field, with the enclosure of the goddess Ishtar. These parts and the district are all Umk"

This too was the work of Gilgamesh, the king, who knew the countries of the world. He was wise, he saw mysteries and knew secret things, he brought us a tale of the days before the flood. He made a long journey, he was tired, exhausted from work, and on his way back he engraved the whole story on a stone.

THE DEATH OF GILGAMESH

The fate that the father of the gods, Enlil of the mountain, had decreed for Gilgamesh was fulfilled, "In the underworld the darkness will show him a light: of humanity, all that is known, no one will leave a monument for generations to come and compare with his. Heroes, sages, like the new moon have their waxing and waning. Men will say, 'Who has ever ruled with power and power like him?' As in the dark month, the month of shadows, so without him there is no light. O Gilgamesh, this was the meaning of your dream. The kingdom was given to you, such was your destiny, eternal life was not your destiny. Therefore do not be sad in heart, do not be grieved or oppressed; he has given you the power to bind and loosen, to be the darkness and light of humanity. He has given unparalleled supremacy over the people, victories in battles from which no fugitive returns, in raids and assaults from which there is no going back. But don't abuse this power, treat rightly your servants in the palace, treat rightly before the face of the sun."

    The king has gone to bed and will not rise again,
    The Lord of Kullab will not rise again;
    He has overcome evil, he will never come back;
    Though he had a strong arm, he won't get up;
    He had wisdom and a beautiful face, he will never come back;
    He went to the mountain, he will never come back;
    On the bed of fate he lies, he will not rise again,
    In front of the sofa of many colors he will never come back.

    The people of the city, great and small, are not silent; they raise, the lament, raise all men in flesh and blood the lament. Destiny has spoken; like a fish on a hook he lies stretched out on the bed, like a gazelle caught in a noose. Inhuman Namtar is heavy on him, Namtar who has neither hands nor feet, who drinks no water and eats no meat.

    For Gilgamesh, son of Ninsun, they weighed their offerings; his dear wife, his son, his concubine, his wife his musicians, his jester, and his whole house; his servants, his administrators, all who lived in the palace weighed theirs offerings for Gilgamesh, son of Ninsun, the heart of Uruk. They weighed their offerings in Ereshkigal, the Queen of Death, and to all the gods of the dead. In Namtar, which is fate, they weighed the offer. Bread for Ned the Guardian of the Gate, bread for Ningizzida the serpent god, the lord of the Tree of Life; for Dumuzi also, the young shepherd, for Enki and Ninki, for Endukugga and Nindukugga, for Enmul and Nimnul, all ancestral deities, ancestors of Enlil. A feast for Shulpae, the god of the banquet. For Samuqan, god of herds, to mother Ninhursag, and the gods of creation in the place of creation, for the army of heaven, priest and priestess weighed the offering of the dead.

Gilgamesh, the son of Ninsun, lies in the grave. At the place of the offerings he weighed the bread offering, at the place of libation he poured the wine. In those days Lord Gilgamesh, son of Ninsun, the king departed, unparalleled, unparalleled among men, who did not neglect Enlil, his master. O Gilgamesh, lord of Kullab, great is your praise.

GLOSSARY OF NAMES

AD AD: Storm-, rain-, and weather-god.

ANUNNAKI; Usually gods of the underworld, judges of the dead and offspring of Anu.

ANSHAN: A district of Elam in south-west Persia; probably the source of supplies of wood for making bows. Gilgamesh has a bow of Anshan'.

ANTUM: Wife of Anu.

ANU: Sumerian An; father of gods, and god of the firmament, the 'great above'. In the Sumerian cosmogony there was, first of all, the primeval sea, from which was born the cosmic mountain consisting of heaven, 'An', and earth, 'Ki'; they were separated by Enlil, then An carried off the heavens, and Enlil the earth. Ann later retreated more and more into the background; he had an important temple in Umk.

APSU: The Abyss; the primeval waters under the earth; in the later mythology of the Enuma Elish, more particularly the sweet water which mingled with the bitter waters of the sea and with a third watery element, perhaps cloud, from which the first gods were engendered. The waters of Apsu were thought of as held immobile underground by the 'spell' of Ea in a death-like sleep.

ARURU: A goddess of creation, she created Enkidu from clay in the image of Anu.

AY A: The dawn, the bride of the Sun God Shamash.

BELIT-SHER1: Scribe and recorder of the underworld gods:

BULL of HEAVEN: A personification of drought created by Anu for Ishtar.

DILMUN: The Sumerian paradise, perhaps the Persian Gulf; some-times described as 'the place where the sun rises' and 'the Land of the Living'; the scene of a Sumerian creation myth and the place where the deified Sumerian hero of the flood, Ziusudra, was taken by the gods to live for ever.

DUMUZI: The Sumerian form of Tammuz; a god of vegetation and fertility, and so of the underworld, also called 'the Shepherd and 'lord of the sheepfolds'. As the companion of Ningizzida 'to all eternity' he stands at the gate of heaven. In the Sumerian 'Descent of Inanna' he is the husband of the goddess Inanna, the Sumerian counterpart of Ishtar. According to the Sumerian King-List Gilgamesh was descended from 'Dumuzi a shepherd'.

EA: Sumerian Enki; god of the sweet waters, also of wisdom, a patron of arts and one of the creators of mankind, towards whom he is usually well-disposed. The chief god of Eridu, where he had a temple, he lived 'in the deep'; his ancestry is uncertain, but he was probably a child of Anu.

EANNA: The temple precinct in Urtik sacred to Anu and Ishtar.

EGALMAH: The 'Great Palace' in Uruk, the home of the goddess Ninsun, the mother of Gilgamesh.

ENDUSUGGA: With Nindukugga, Sumerian gods living in the underworld; parents of Enlil.

ENKIDU: Moulded by Arum, goddess of creation, out of clay is the image and 'of the essence of Anu', the sky-god, and of Ninurta the war-god. The companion of Gilgamesh, he is wild or natural reran; he was later considered a patron or god of anima b and may have been the hero of another cycle.

ENLIL: God of earth, wind, and the universal air, ultimately spirit; the executive of Anu. In the Sumerian cosmogony he was born of the union of An heaven, and Ki earth. These he separated, and he then carried off earth as his portion. In later times he supplanted Anu as chief god. He was the patron of the city of Nippur.

ENMUL: See Endukugga.

ENNUGI: God of irrigation and inspector of Canals.

ENUMA ELLISH: The Semitic creation epic which describes the creation of the gods, the defeat of the powers of chaos by the young god Marduk, and the creation of man from the blood of Kingu, the defeated champion of chaos. The title is taken from the first words of the epic 'When on high'.

ERESHKIGAL: The Queen of the underworld, a counterpart of Persephone; probably once a sky-goddess. In the Sumerian cosmogony she was carried off to the underworld after the separation of heaven and earth.

ETANA: Legendary king of Kish who reigned after the flood; in the epic which bears his name he was carried to heaven on the back of an eagle.

GILGAMESH: The hero of the Epic; son of the goddess Ninsun and of a priest of Kullab, fifth king of Uruk after the flood, famous as a great builder and as a judge of the dead. A cycle of epic poems has collected round his name.

HANISH: A divine herald of storm and bad weather.

HUMBABA: Also Huwawa; a guardian of the cedar forest who opposes Gilgamesh and is killed by him and Enkidu. A nature divinity, perhaps an Anatolian, Elamite, or Syrian god.

IGIGI: Collective name for the great gods of heaven.

IRKALLA: Another name for Ereshkigal; the Queen of the underworld.

ISHTAR: Sumerian Inanna; the goddess of love and fertility, also goddess of war, called the Queen of Heaven. She is the daughter of Anu and patroness of Uruk, where she has a temple.

ISHULLANA: The: gardener of Anu, once loved by Ishtar whom he rejected; he was turned by her into a mole or frog.

KI: The earth.

KULLAS:Part of Uruk.

LUGULEANDA: Third king of the post-diluvian dynasty of Uruk, a god and shepherd, and hero of a cycle of Sumerian poems; protector of Gilgamesh.

MAGAN: A land to the west of Mesopotamia, sometimes Egypt or Arabia, and sometimes the land of the dead, the underworld:

MAGILUM: Uncertain meaning, perhaps 'the boat of the dead'.

MAMMETUM: Ancestral goddess responsible for destinies.

MAN-SCORPION: Guardian, with a similar female monster, of the mountain into which the sun descends at nightfall. Shown on sealings and ivory inlays as a figure with the upper part of the body human and the lower part ending in a scorpion's mil. According to the Enuma Elish created by the primeval waters in order to fight the gods.

MASHU: The word means 'twins' in the Akkadian language. A mountain with twin peaks into which the sun descends at nightfall and from which it returns at dawn. Sometimes thought of as Lebanon and Anti -Lebanon.

NAMTAR: Fate, destiny in its evil aspect; pictured as a demon of the underworld, also a messenger and chief minister of Ereshkigal; a bringer of disease and pestilence.

NEDU: See Ned.

NERGAL: Underworld god, sometimes the husband of Ereshkigal, he is the subject of an Akkadian poem which describes his translation from heaven to the underworld; plague-god.

NETI: The Sumerian form of Nedu, the chief gatekeeper in the underworld.

NINDUKUGGA: With Endukugga, parental gods living in the underworld:

NINGAL: Wife of the Moon God and mother of the Sun.

NINGIESU: An earlier form of Ninurta; god of irrigation and fertility, he had a field near Lagash where all sorts of plants flourished; he was the child of a she-goat.

NINGIZZIDA: Also Gizzida; a fertility god, addressed as 'Lord of the Tree of Life'; sometimes he is a serpent with human head, but later he was a god of healing and magic; the companion of Tammuz, with whom he stood at the gate of heaven.

NINHURSAG: Sumerian mother-goddess; one of the four principal Sumerian gods with An, Enlil, and Enki; sometimes the wife of Enki, she created all vegetation. The name means 'the Mother'; she is also called 'Nintu', lady of birth, and IG, the earth.

NINKI: The 'mother' of Enlil, probably a form of Ninhursag.

NINLIL: Goddess of heaven, earth, and air and in one aspect of the underworld; wife of Enlil and mother of the Moon; worshipped with Enlil in Nippur.

NINSUM The mother of Gilgamesh, a minor goddess whose house was in Uruk; she was noted for wisdom, and was the wife of Lugulbaada.

NINURTA: The later forth of Ningirsu; a warrior and god of war, a herald, the south wind, and god of wells and irrigation. According to one poem he once dammed up the bitter waters of the underworld and conquered various monsters.

NISABA: Goddess of grain.

NISIR: Probably means 'Mountain of Salvation'; sometimes identified with the Pir Oman Gudrun range south of the lower Zab, or with the biblical Ararat north of Lake Van.

PUZUR-AMURRI: The steersman of Utnapishtim during the flood.

SAMUQ AN: God of cattle;

SEVEN SAGES: Wise men who brought civilization to the seven oldest cities of Mesopotamia.

SHAMASH: Sumerian Utu; the sun; for the Sumerians he was principally the judge and law-giver with some fertility attributes. For the Semites he was also a victorious warrior, the god of wisdom, the son of Sin, and 'greater than his father'. He was the husband and brother of Ishtar. He is represented with the saw with which he cuts decisions. In the poems 'Shamash' may mean the god, or simply the sun.

SHULLAT : A divine herald of storm and of bad weather.

SHULPAE: A god who presided over feasts and feasting.

SHURRUPAX: Modem Fara, eighteen miles north-west of Uruk; one of the oldest cities of Mesopotamia, and one of the five named by the Sumerians as having existed before the flood. The home of the hero of the flood story.

SIDURI: The divine wine-maker and brewer; she lives on the shore of the sea (perhaps the Mediterranean), in the garden of the sun. Her name in the Hurrian language means 'young woman' and she may be a form of Ishtar.

SILILI: The mother of the stallion; a divine mare?

SIN: Sumerian Nama, the moon. The chief Sumerian astral deity, the father of Utu-Shamash, the sun, and of Ishtar. Ills parents were Enlil and Ninlil. His chief temple was in Ur.

TAMMUZ: Sumerian Dunuzi; the dying god of vegetation, bewailed by Ishtar, the subject of laments and litanies. In an Akkadian poem Ishtar descends to the underworld in search of her young husband Tammuz; but in the Sumerian poem on which this is based it is Inanna herself who is responsible for sending Dumuzi to the under- world because of his pride and as a hostage for her own safe return.

UBARA-TUTU: A king of Shurrupak and father of Utnapishtim The only king of Kish named in the prediluvian Ring-List, apart from Utnapishtim.

URSHANABI: Old Babylonian Sursunabu; the boatman of Utnapishtim who ferries daily across the waters of death which divide the garden of the sun from the paradise where Utnapishtim lives for ever (the Sumerian Dilmun). By accepting Gilgamesh as a passenger he forfeits this right, and accompanies Gilgamesh back to Uruk instead.

URUK: Biblical Erech, modem Warka, in southern Babylonia between Fara (Shutrupak) and Ur. Shown by excavation to have been an important city from very early times, with great temples to the gods Anu and Ishtar. Traditionally the enemy of the city of Kish, and after the flood the seat of a dynasty of kings, among whom Gilga- mesh was the fifth and most famous.

UTNAPISHTIM: Old Babylonian Utanapishtim, Sumerian Ziusu-dra; in the Sumerian poems he is a wise king and priest of Shurrupak ; in the Akkadian sources he is a wise citizen of Shurrupak. He is the son of Ubara Tutu, and his name is usually translated, 'He Who Saw Life'. He is the protege of the god Ea, by whose connivance he Sur- vives the Hood, with his family and with 'the seed of all living creatures'; afterwards he is taken by the gods to live for ever at 'the mouth of the rivers' and given the epithet 'Faraway'; or according to the Sumerians he lives in Dihnun where the sun rises

Made in the USA
Monee, IL
09 December 2021

84515902R00033